WORD PROBLEMS

USING

OPERATIONS AND ALGEBRAIC THINKING

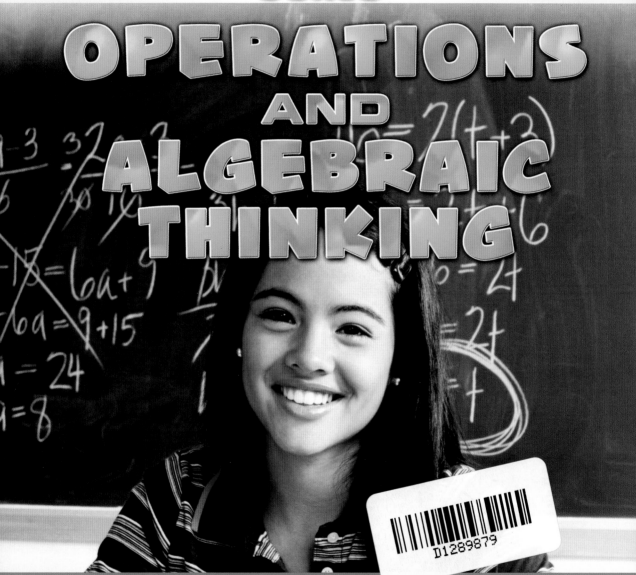

MASTERING MATH WORD PROBLEMS

Zella Williams and
Rebecca Wingard-Nelson

Enslow Publishing
101 W. 23rd Street
Suite 240
New York, NY 10011
USA

enslow.com

Published in 2017 by Enslow Publishing, LLC.
101 W. 23rd Street, Suite 240, New York, NY 10011

Library of Congress Cataloging-in-Publication Data

Names: Williams, Zella, author. | Wingard-Nelson, Rebecca, author.
Title: Word problems using operations and algebraic thinking / Zella Williams and Rebecca Wingard-Nelson.
Description: New York, NY : Enslow Publishing, 2017. | Series: Mastering math word problems | Includes bibliographical references and index.
Identifiers: LCCN 2016032320| ISBN 9780766082700 (library bound) | ISBN 9780766082694 (6 pack) | ISBN 9780766082687 (pbk.)
Subjects: LCSH: Algebraic topology—Juvenile literature. | Cohomology operations—Juvenile literature. | Algebra—Juvenile literature. | Word problems (Mathematics)—Juvenile literature.
Classification: LCC QA612.14 .W56 2017 | DDC 512.9—dc23
LC record available at https://lccn.loc.gov/2016032320

Printed in China

To Our Readers: We have done our best to make sure all websites in this book were active and appropriate when we went to press. However, the author and the publisher have no control over and assume no liability for the material available on those websites or on any websites they may link to. Any comments or suggestions can be sent by e-mail to customerservice@enslow.com.

Portions of this book originally appeared in the book *Amusement Park Word Problems Starring Pre-Algebra*.

Photo Credits: Cover, p. 1 Digital Vision/Getty Images; pp. 3, 21 Kelly/Mooney Photography/Corbis Documentary/Getty Images; p. 4 JGI/Jamie Grill/Blend Images/Getty Images; p. 5 (book) Maximilian Laschon/Shutterstock.com; p. 7 Toru Yamanaka/AFP/ Getty Images; p. 10 Lakov Filimonov/Shutterstock.com; p. 11 Sean Pavone/Shutterstock. com; p. 12 Misunseo/Shutterstock.com; p. 14 Envision/Corbis Documentary/Getty Images; p. 16 rustyl3599/iStock/Thinkstock; p. 19 © Ryan McGinnis/Alamy Stock Photo; p. 23 © Cathy Melloan/Alamy Stock Photo; p. 26 Purestock/Getty Images; p. 27 David Cumming/Corbis Documentary/Getty Images; p. 29 © JHP Attractions/Alamy Stock Photo; p. 31 ymgerman/Shutterstock.com; p. 34 Andyworks/E+/Getty Images; p. 35 Juergen Richter/LOOK-foto/Getty Images; p. 37 Pavel L Photo and Video/Shutterstock. com; p. 39 © Cernan Elias/Alamy Stock Photo; p. 41 Jeff Greenberg/Universal Images Group/Getty Images; p. 43 © kevin wheal surrey/Alamy Stock Photo; p. 47 bluelela/ Shutterstock.com; cover and interior pages icons and graphics Shutterstock.com: Anna_leni (owl), Draze Design (pad and pencil), RedlineVector (light bulb), Yuri Gayvoronskiy (eyes), james Weston (scrambled numbers), Ratoca (thumbs up), BeRad (magnifying glass).

Contents

Keep a word problem notebook. You can look back at strategies you've used for other problems to help you solve new ones.

Word Problems: Problem Solved!

! Tips for Solving Word Problems

Word problems might be part of your homework, on a test, or in your life. These tips can help you solve them, no matter where they show up.

Be positive!

When you get a problem right the first time, that's great! When you don't get a problem right the first time, don't worry. If you learn from your mistakes, you will become better at solving word problems.

Don't wait to get help!

New problems build on old ones. If you don't understand today's problem, tomorrow's problem will be even harder to understand.

In some problems, you will see clue spotters. A magnifying glass will help you spy clue words in the problem.

Practice!

The more you practice anything, the better you become at it. Do your homework problems as that's your practice for solving word problems.

Move on!

If you get stuck, move on to the next problem. If you work on the ones you know how to solve first, you'll feel more confident. Plus, you won't miss the ones you know because you ran out of time.

Ask questions!

When someone is helping you, asking good questions tells the person what you don't understand. If you don't ask questions, you will never get answers!

Take a breather!

If you have tried everything you can think and are getting frustrated, take a break. Take a deep breath. Stretch your arms and legs. Get a drink of water or a snack. Then come back and try again.

Don't give up!

The first time you try to solve a word problem, you might come up with an answer that does not make sense or that you know is not right. Don't give up! Check your math. Try solving the problem a different way. If you quit, you won't learn.

! Follow the Steps

Word problems may seem hard. They can be solved by following four easy steps, though.

? Here's a problem.

The greatest speed of the fastest steel roller coaster is 134 mph (216 km/h). The greatest speed of the fastest wooden roller coaster is 78 mph (126 km/h). How much faster is the steel roller coaster's greatest speed?

Step 1 Read and understand the problem.

Read the problem carefully. Ask yourself questions, such as:

What do you know?

The greatest speed of the fastest steel roller coaster is 134 mph. The greatest speed of the fastest wooden roller coaster is 78 mph.

What are you trying to find?

How much faster the steel roller coaster is than the wooden roller coaster.

Modern steel roller coasters like this one move pretty fast. They are made to give riders the biggest thrills their dollars can buy!

What kind of problem is this?

You want to know the difference between the two greatest speeds. Problems that find a difference are subtraction problems.

Step 2 Make a plan.

Some problems tell you how they should be solved. They may say "draw a picture" or "write an equation." For other problems, you will need to make your own plan. Most problems can be solved in more than one way. Some plans you might try are:

Look for a pattern   **Write an equation**
Draw a picture   **Use a model**
Estimate   **Break it apart**

How can you solve this problem?

Let's write an equation. That's our plan.

Step 3 Solve the problem.

It is time to do the math!

If you find that your plan is not working, make a new plan. Don't give up the first time.

Let's write an equation.

Use the numbers from the problem to write a subtraction equation. Start with the bigger number, 134 mph. Subtract the smaller number, 78 mph, to find the difference.

$134 - 78 = 56$

The greatest speed of the steel roller coaster is 56 mph faster than the greatest speed of the wooden roller coaster.

 ## Step 4 Look back.

The problem is solved!

But you aren't finished yet. Take a good look at your answer.

Does it make sense? Did you include the units? Did you use the right numbers to begin? Estimate or use a different operation to check your math.

Is there another way you can solve this problem?

Yes. You could use a place value drawing to find the difference between 78 and 134.

Clue Words

Clue words are words that give you hints about what the problem wants you to solve. Clue words can help you figure out which operation to use to solve problems.

Here's a problem.

In one amusement park, 21 of the rides are water rides and 16 are not water rides. How many rides are there combined?

In this problem the clue word "**combined**" tells you to add the water rides and the non-water rides. Some other clue words that tell you a problem might use addition are: **add**, **sum**, **total**, **plus**, **more**, **together**, **increase**, and **both**.

Here's another problem.

At one amusement park, 21 of the rides are water rides and 16 rides are not water rides. How many more rides are water rides than non-water rides?

People sit on rafts or floats for some water rides.

In this problem the clue words "**how many more**" tell you to find the difference between the number of water rides and the number of non-water rides. Problems that find the difference between two values, such as rides, are subtraction problems. Some other clue words that tell you a problem might use subtraction are: **subtract**, **difference**, **take away**, **how much less**, **how much farther**, **remain**, **left**, **fewer**, and **compare**.

See if you can spot the clue words in this problem.

Each ride on the Ferris wheel takes 3 tickets. If 6 people want to ride the Ferris wheel together, how many tickets do they need?

In this problem, the clue word "**each**" tells you that you know the quantity of tickets for one ride. In this case it takes 3 tickets for one ride.

The first Ferris wheel opened in 1893 for the Chicago World's Fair. Today you can ride one at most amusement parks around the country.

You need to find the quantity of tickets for 6 rides. This is a multiplication problem. Some other clue words that tell you a problem might use multiplication are: at, every, multiply, of, per, product, rate, times, and twice.

Here's an example.

What do the clue words tell you in this problem?

A family of 6 people used 18 tickets to ride the Ferris wheel once. How many tickets does the Ferris wheel cost per ride?

You are given the number of tickets (18) for 6 people to ride. The clue word "**per**" tells you to find the number of tickets for one person to ride. This is division. Some other clue words that tell you a problem might use division are: **divided**, **each**, **equally**, **evenly**, **every**, **half**, and **split**.

Amusement parks sell thousands of tickets to park visitors every year.

Opposite Problems

Let's look at the facts from the Ferris wheel problems.
Each ride takes 3 tickets. Six people want to ride.
Six rides take 18 tickets.
Using these facts, you can write two types of problems.

Multiplication:

6 rides × 3 tickets each = 18 tickets

Division:

18 tickets ÷ 6 rides = 3 tickets each

Because they are related, operations that are the
opposite sometimes use the same clue words, such as
"per" and "each." The clue words will help you get
started, but you must understand what is happening in
the problem and what question is being asked.

More Than One Operation

You can see that we use addition, subtraction,
multiplication, and division to solve problems.
Addition, subtraction, multiplication, and division are
called operations. Some problems have a combination
of all of these operations.

So how do you know which parts to solve first?

You need to follow the order of operations. The order
of operations is a set of rules that tells you the order in
which to perform operations, such as addition
or multiplication.

The order of operations is:

1. Compute any numbers inside parentheses first.
2. Multiply or divide from left to right.
3. Add or subtract from left to right.

Pizza is a great way to learn about fractions. One slice of a pizza that is cut into four slices is one-fourth of the whole pizza! You can also add the slices like we are doing for the problem on this page.

 Here's the problem.

The Cleaver family found a food stand that sold whole pizzas and pizza by the slice. They bought 2 whole pizzas that contained 4 slices each and another slice by itself. How many slices of pizza did they buy in all?

 Read and understand.

What do you know?
The Cleavers bought 2 whole pizzas with 4 slices in each pizza. They also bought 1 single slice.

What are you trying to find?
The number of slices the Cleavers bought in all.

Plan.

Let's write an equation.

Solve.

Write an equation to match the problem.
Let's write it in words first.

number of Pizzas	times	slices in each pizza	plus	one more slice	equals	slices in all
2	×	4	+	1	=	slices in all

The order of operations tells you to multiply first, then add.

Multiply first. 2 pizzas × 4 slices each = 8 slices.

Then add. 8 slices + 1 more slice = 9 slices in all.

The Cleavers bought 9 slices of pizza in all.

 ## Look back.

Does the order of operations make sense with the problem?

Yes. You must find the number of slices in the two pizzas before you add the extra piece.

What happens if you add before you multiply?

Use parentheses around the addition part to show you want to add first. To solve $2 \times (4 + 1)$, first add inside the parentheses. $4 + 1 = 5$. Then multiply. $2 \times 5 = 10$. The equation $2 \times (4 + 1) = 10$ does not equal $2 \times 4 + 1 = 9$.

Draw a Picture

You can draw a picture to see that you can multiply numbers in any order and the answers will be the same. You can also add numbers in any order and the answers will be the same.

Here's a problem.

Sonya won a stuffed snake at the balloon game. The game board had 10 rows of balloons with 16 balloons in each row. How many balloons were on the game board?

Can you count how many balloons there are in this balloon game?

Read and understand.

What do you know?

The game board had 10 rows of balloons with 16 balloons in each row.

What are you trying to find?

The number of balloons on the game board.

Plan.

Let's draw a picture.

Solve.

Draw a simple picture.

Represent each balloon with an X. There are 10 rows with 16 in each row.

To find the total number of balloons, you can count each X, you can add the Xs in each row (16 + 16 . . .), or you can multiply 10 rows by 16 balloons in each row.

$10 \times 16 = 160$

There were 160 balloons on the game board.

 Look back.

Does it matter if you multiply 10 $\times$ 16 or 16 $\times$ 10?

No. In multiplication, the order of the factors does not matter. You can use the picture to see that this is true. If you turn your picture sideways so there are 16 rows with 10 in each row, does the total change? No.

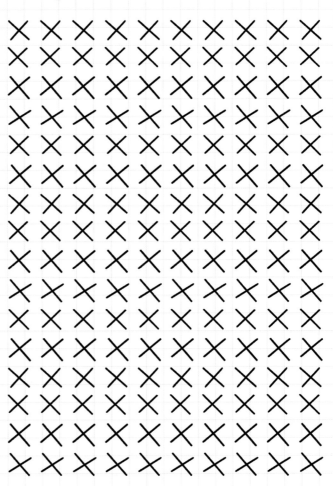

Different Ways to Solve Word Problems

❗ Using Mental Math

Some word problems can be solved using mental math. In an addition problem, it doesn't matter in what order you add the numbers in the problem. You can group the numbers together to make them easier to add in your head.

❓ Here's the problem.

Anton rode the Gravitron 5 times by himself, 16 times with his friends, plus 4 more times with his little sister.
How many times did he ride in all?

The Gravitron spins fast enough to push riders against the inside walls. It uses the same force you feel when you are riding in a car that goes quickly around a bend in the road.

Read and understand.

What do you know?

Anton rode the Gravitron:

5 times alone

16 times with friends

4 times with his sister

What are you trying to find?

The number of times Anton rode the Gravitron in all.

Plan.

Let's use mental math.

Solve.

There are three numbers to add: $5 + 16 + 4$

You can group the numbers to make them easier to add in your head.

Think: $5 + 16 + 4$

What's the easiest combination to add first? $16 + 4 = 20$

Think: $5 + 20$ $5 + 20 = 25$

Anton rode the Gravitron 25 times in all.

Look back.

Is the math correct?

Use a paper and pencil to check the math. This time, add from left to right.

$5 + 16 + 4$: $5 + 16 = 21$ $21 + 4 = 25$

Tricky Questions

Sometimes a word problem does not have any obvious clue words to tell you the operation. You have to think through what is being said to solve the problem.

? *Here's an example.*

Sabrina rode on the log flume 8 times. She stayed dry on 0 of her log flume rides. On how many of her log flume rides did Sabrina get wet?

Log flume rides are kind of like a roller coaster on water. They are fun, but you might get a little wet!

Read and understand.

What do you know?

Sabrina rode the log flume 8 times.

She stayed dry on 0 of her log flume rides.

What are you trying to find?

The number of rides that got Sabrina wet.

What hidden or tricky information is in the problem?

You are given the number of total rides and the number of rides Sabrina stayed dry. But then the problem asks you how many times she got wet, which was not a value you were given. You must know that wet and dry are opposites. Sabrina either stayed dry or got wet.

What kind of problem is this?

There is no clue word, so decide what happens in the problem. Sabrina had a total of 8 log flume rides. She stayed dry on none of the rides. You want to find the remaining number of rides. You need to subtract.

Plan.

Let's write an equation.

Solve.

Use the numbers from the problem to write a subtraction equation.

Total rides – dry rides = wet rides

$8 - 0 = 8$

Sabrina got wet on 8 of her log flume rides.

Look back.

Check your subtraction by using addition.

Add the answer (8) to the number you subtracted (0).

If the sum (8) is the number you started with, then your answer is correct. $8 + 0 = 8$

Too Much Information

Some problems give more information than you need. You need to ignore that information to solve the problem.

Here's the problem.

Bridget won 6 goldfish by throwing balls into fishbowls. She paid $1.00 per ball for 12 balls. How much did Bridget spend at the game?

Read and understand.

What do you know?

Bridget won 6 goldfish. She paid to throw 12 balls. Each ball cost $1.00.

What are you trying to find?

The amount of money Bridget spent at the fishbowl game.

The goldfish game is tricky. The mouths of the bowls are only a little wider than the ball you toss. This makes it hard to win!

What do you need to know to solve the problem? Which information is extra?

How many balls she paid for, and how much she paid for each one. You do not need to know that she won 6 goldfish. It will not help you solve the problem.

Are there any clue words?

Yes. The clue word "**per**" tells you this is multiplication or division. You know the cost of one ball ($1.00). You want to find the cost of more than one ball (12). This is multiplication.

Plan.

Let's use what we know about ones.

Solve.

When you multiply or divide any number by 1, the number stays the same. The cost of one ball is $1.00, or $1, so the cost of 12 balls is 12×1, or $12.00.

Bridget spent $12.00 at the fishbowl game.

Look back.

Could you have solved this problem another way?

You could draw a picture.

Draw 12 circles for the balls Bridget paid for. Write $1 on each ball for the cost. Now count the number of dollars. There are 12.

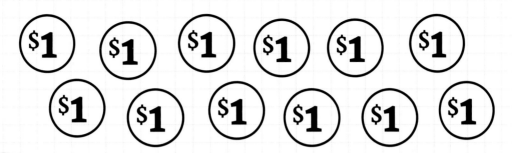

! Find a Pattern

Math problems can often involve patterns. Word problems are no different. Tables can help you find patterns in a problem.

? Here's the problem.

Adrian's mom waved every time he passed her on the carousel. After one ride, he passed her 12 times. After two rides, he passed her 24 times. Adrian took 6 rides. How many times did he pass his mom?

Read and understand.

What do you know?
After 1 ride, Adrian passed his mom 12 times. After 2 rides, he passed her 24 times. He rode 6 times.

What are you trying to find?
The number of times Adrian passed his mom.

Plan.

Let's make a table.

The modern carousel had its beginnings in traditions from hundreds of years ago. Mounted knights would ride their horses in a circle while tossing a ball to one another. It took great skill.

Solve.

Make a table that organizes what you know.

A table can make it easier to see a pattern.

number of rides	1	2	3	4	5	6
number of times past mom	12	24	36	48	60	72

For each ride, Adrian passed his mom 12 times. To find the total number of times he passed her, you can add 12 more passes for each ride, or you can multiply the number of rides by 12.

$6 \times 12 = 72$

Adrian passed his mom 72 times.

Look back.

Does the answer match the question? Did you include the units?

Yes.

Expressions in Math

! Write an Expression

Expressions can be numbers or a combination of numbers and operations. Expressions do not use the equal sign.

? Here's the problem.

Hans stood in line for 14 minutes to ride the pirate ship. His ride was 6 minutes long. Write an expression that shows how to find the difference in minutes between Hans's time in line and his time on the ride.

The pirate ship ride is not for the faint of heart. It swings the rider back and forth like a pendulum. The rider feels weightless for a moment at the top of the swing before heading down to swing the other way.

Read and understand.

What do you know?

Hans stood in line for 14 minutes.

His ride lasted 6 minutes.

What are you trying to find?

An expression that shows how to find the difference in minutes between the time in line and the time on the ride.

Are there any clue words?

Yes. The word "**difference**" tells you this is a subtraction problem.

Plan.

Let's write an expression.

Solve.

Start with the number of minutes Hans stood in line, 14. Write the subtraction sign to show you must subtract. Then write the number of minutes Hans rode on the pirate ship, or 6 minutes.

$$\begin{array}{r} 14 \\ -\ 6 \\ \hline \end{array}$$

The expression that shows how to find the difference between Hans's time in line and his time on the ride is $14 - 6$.

Look back.

Did you answer the right question?

Yes

Hans spent 8 minutes longer in line than he did on the ride. Why is 8 minutes not the answer here?

The problem does *not* ask you for the difference. It asks you to *write an expression* that shows how to find the difference. The answer 8 minutes does not show that you use subtraction.

Variable Expressions

You can use a letter or symbol in an expression to represent a number you don't know. The letter or symbol is called a variable. When you use letters in an expression or equation, you are doing algebra. Algebra is trickier than basic arithmetic, because you are solving for an unknown quantity.

Here's the problem.

Passes to an amusement park cost $39.75 each. Write an expression to show the cost of a number of passes. Use the letter *p* to represent the number of passes.

FASTPASS®
Return Anytime Between
1:30 PM
AND
2:30 PM

Riders must be at least 48" (122cm) to experience Rock n Roller Coaster.

Another FASTPASS® ticket will be available after 1:30pm
THU MAY 01

What if a pass costs $10 and you need to buy three? Use the information in this section to help you solve the problem.

Read and understand.

What do you know?

The cost of one pass is $39.75.

What are you trying to find?

An expression that shows the cost of a number of passes.

Are there any clue words in the problem?

Yes. The clue word "**each**" tells you this is either a multiplication or division problem. The problem gives you the cost of one, and you need to show the cost of a number of passes. This is a multiplication problem.

Plan.

Let's write an expression.

Solve.

To find the cost of any number of passes, multiply the cost of one pass by the number of passes.

Cost of one pass times number of passes

$39.75 \times p$

An expression for the cost of a number of passes is $39.75 \times p$.

Look back.

Is there another way to write the expression?

Yes. When you are using a variable, you can drop the multiplication symbol. $39.75 \times p$ can be written as $39.75p$.

From Expressions to Equations

Once you figure out the expression you need to solve a problem, you can create an equation by adding the equal sign and solving the problem. Keep in mind that some problems have more than one question. Problems with more than one question must have more than one answer.

? Here's the problem.

Nhu went down the giant slide 6 times, got a drink, then went down the slide some more times. Write an expression for how many times Nhu went down the slide in all. Then find the total number of times she went down the slide if she went down 10 more times after her drink.

Can you count how many people are racing down this giant slide?

Read and understand.

What do you know?

Nhu went down the giant slide 6 times, then she went down some more times.

What are you trying to find?

Two things: an expression for the total number of times Nhu went down the slide, and the total number of times if she went down the slide 10 times after her drink.

Plan.

Let's write the expression, then use the expression to find the answer.

Solve.

Use the letter *s* to stand for the number of times Nhu went down the slide after she had a drink.

First Nhu went down the slide 6 times		Then she went down more times
6	+	*s*

Nhu went down the slide 6 *s* times in all.
If Nhu went down the slide 10 times after her drink, put 10 into the expression in place of the *s*. Then add.

$6 + 10 = 16.$

Nhu went down the slide 16 times in all.

Look back.

If Nhu went down the slide 6 times after her drink, would the answer change?

The expression $(6 + s)$ would be the same, but the total would be different $(6 + 6 = 12)$.

Related Equations

Expressions do not have an equal sign. They express a mathematical idea, but they do not solve it. To solve a problem you need an equation. An equation has an equal sign. Sometimes a word problem might ask you to come up with related equations that can help solve a problem. Related equations are often inverse operations, like multiplication and division or addition and subtraction.

Here's the problem.

There are 64 people riding in the bumper cars. Each car has 2 riders. There are 32 cars. Write a division equation that matches this problem, then write a related multiplication equation.

Read and understand.

What do you know?

There are 64 people riding in the bumper cars. Each car has 2 riders. There are 32 cars.

Bumper cars are made to fit one or two people in them. Riders drive around and try to bump other cars.

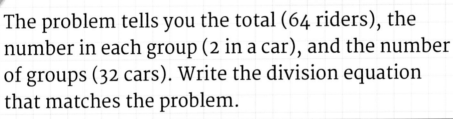

What are you trying to find?
You are finding two equations, one division and one multiplication.

Plan.

Let's write the equations.

Solve.

The problem tells you the total (64 riders), the number in each group (2 in a car), and the number of groups (32 cars). Write the division equation that matches the problem.

total riders	÷	riders in one car	=	number of cars
64	÷	2	=	32

One possible division equation is $64 \div 2 = 32$.
Now write a related multiplication equation.

riders in car	×	number of cars	=	total riders
2	×	32	=	64

So, a related multiplication equation is $2 \times 32 = 64$.

Look back.

Did you answer the right question?

Yes. The problem asked for two equations, a division equation and a related multiplication equation.

Solution Equations

Related equations can help you solve word problems.

Here's the problem.

Two people can ride in a waterslide raft together if they weigh less than 225 pounds total. Doug, who weighs 115 pounds, got into a raft. Eric got into the raft with Doug. Together, they weighed 220 pounds. How much does Eric weigh?

Waterslide rafts are typically made from plastic and inflated with air.

Read and understand.

What do you know?

Doug weighs 115 pounds.

Together, Doug and Eric weigh 220 pounds.

What are you trying to find?

Eric's weight.

Are there any clue words?

Yes. The word "**together**" shows addition is happening.

Plan.

Let's write an equation.

Solve.

Equations that match what happens in a problem are sometimes called situation equations. Write a situation equation for the problem.

Doug's weight	+	Eric's weight	=	weight together
115	+	w	=	220

Equations that are related to a situation equation, but are easier to solve, are sometimes called solution equations. Write a related solution equation that has the letter by itself on one side of the equal sign.

$115 + w = 220$ is related to $\quad w = 220 - 115$

Now solve the related equation by subtracting.

$105 = 220 - 115$, so $w = 105$.

Eric weighs 105 pounds.

Look back.

Check your answer.

Put your answer, 105, into the original situation equation, then add.

$115 + 105 = 220$. The answer is correct.

Pictures and Equations

A picture or diagram can help you write or solve equations

Here's the problem.

In one mirror maze, there are 84 walls. Some of the walls are mirrored glass. The remaining 22 walls are clear glass. How many mirrored glass walls are there?

Mirror mazes use lots of mirrors to confuse people trying to find their way out of the maze.

Read and understand.

What do you know?

There are 84 walls in all.

Some of the walls are mirrored glass.

There are 22 walls of clear glass.

What are you trying to find?

The number of mirrored glass walls.

Plan.

Let's write an equation.

Solve.

The problem gives the number of total walls and clear walls. You do not know the number of mirrored walls. Use the letter m for the number you do not know.

total walls	−	mirrored walls	=	clear walls
84	−	m	=	22

To solve this equation, let's make a place-value drawing. Start with 84 to represent the total walls.

Cross off the squares and rectangles representing the place values until there are only 22 remaining. **How much did you cross off?** You crossed off 6 tens rectangles and 2 ones squares.

There are 62 mirrored walls.

Look back.

Is there another way you could solve this problem?

Yes. You could solve the equation, $84 - m = 22$, by using the related equation $84 = 22 + m$, or $84 - 22 = m$. $84 - 22 = 62$, so $m = 62$.

Keep It Equal

You can do the same thing to each side of an equation, and the sides remain equal.

Here's the problem.

You must be at least 54 inches tall to ride the Tilt-A-Whirl without an adult. Jenna needs to grow another 3 inches before she can do this. How tall is Jenna now?

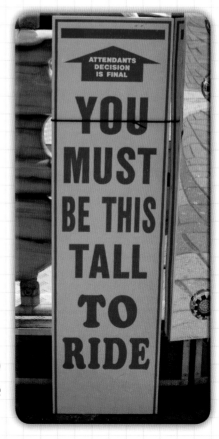

Have you ever seen these signs at an amusement park? They tell you how tall you must be to ride safely. Different rides have different height requirements.

Read and understand.

What do you know?

You must be 54 inches tall to ride without an adult.
Jenna needs to grow 3 inches to ride without an adult.

What are you trying to find?

You are trying to find Jenna's height now.

Plan.

Let's write an equation.

Solve.

Write a situation equation to match the problem.

Jenna's height + 3 inches = height to ride alone

$h + 3 = 54$

You can find an unknown value in an equation by getting the unknown by itself on one side of the equal sign. One way to get the unknown by itself is to do the same operation on each side of an equation.

To get h alone, you can subtract 3 from each side.

$h + 3 = 54$

$h + 3 - 3 = 54 - 3$

$h + 0 = 51$

$h = 51$

Jenna is 51 inches tall.

Look back.

Check your math. Put the answer (51) into the original equation ($h + 3 = 54$). $51 + 3 = 54$

Use a Formula

A formula is a special equation that uses letters to stand for values. Once you have a formula, you can use it to solve for different values that you plug in.

 Here's the problem.

The wave pool is a square pool with a side length of 200 feet. Dai walked the whole way around the wave pool one time. How far did he walk? Use the formula for the perimeter of a square ($P = 4s$).

A wave pool has waves that are like ocean waves, but they are made by a machine and the beach part is made of concrete!

 Read and understand.

What do you know?
The wave pool is a square. Each side is 200 feet long. Dai walked around the pool one time.

What are you trying to find?
You are trying to find how far Dai walked.

How are you told to solve the problem?

Use the formula for the perimeter of a square.

 Plan.

Let's use the formula.

 Solve.

Write the formula. In this formula, P stands for perimeter, or distance around. The letter s stands for the length of one side.

$P = 4s$

Put the numbers you know from the problem into the formula. You know the side length is 200 feet.

$P = 4 \times 200$ Multiply. $4 \times 200 = 800$

$P = 800$

Dai walked 800 feet.

 Look back.

Check the answer.

Since multiplication is repeated addition, you can add the length for each side.

$200 + 200 + 200 + 200 = 800$.

Because this is a formula, you could figure out how far Dai walked for any pool, even if it was bigger or smaller than this pool. Pick any number and try it out!

Use Your Thinking Skills

Some word problems cannot be solved using arithmetic. You need to use only your thinking skills.

 Here's the problem.

Liza, Juno, and Tessa are waiting in line for the chair swing. Liza is directly in front of Juno. Ashe cuts in line directly in front of Tessa. Tessa is somewhere behind Liza. Of the four friends, who is last in line?

When you use your thinking skills, rather than your math skills, to solve a problem, you are using logic. Lots of more advanced math requires logic *and* math skills!

Read and understand.

What do you know?

There are four friends in all: Liza, Juno, Tessa, and Ashe. There are three clues about their order.

1. Liza is directly in front of Juno.

2. Ashe is directly in front of Tessa.

3. Tessa is somewhere behind Liza.

What are you trying to find?

Which of the four friends is last in line.

Plan.

Let's use the clues and thinking skills.

Solve.

The word "directly" means the friends are right next to each other. There are two sets of friends that are next to each other.

Liza is directly in front of Juno. Ashe cuts directly in front of Tessa

Tessa is somewhere behind Liza, so Liza and Juno must be in front of Ashe and Tessa.

The order of the friends is:

Liza, Juno, Ashe, Tessa.

The last friend in line is Tessa.

Look back.

Look back at all of the clues and make sure your answer meets the clues. **Is Liza directly in front of Juno?**

Yes.

Is Ashe directly in front of Tessa? Is Tessa somewhere behind Liza?

Yes.

Remember the Plan

To solve a word problem, follow these steps:

Read and understand the problem.

Know what the problem says and what you need to find. If you don't understand, ask questions before you start.

Make a plan.

Choose the plan that makes the most sense and is easiest for you. Remember, there is usually more than one way to find the right answer.

Solve the problem.

Use the plan. If your first plan isn't working, try a different one. Take a break and come back with a fresh mind.

Look back.

Read the problem again. Make sure your answer makes sense. Check your math. If the answer does not look right, don't give up now! Use what you've learned to go back and try the problem again.

Glossary

addition One of the four basic operations in math; the process of adding two or more numbers together.

algebra A broad part of math that covers many areas, but in this book we are talking about solving for unknowns in expressions, equations, and formulas.

division One of the four basic operations in math; the process of finding out how many times a smaller number is contained within a larger one.

equation A number sentence such as $1 + 1 = 2$, where both expressions on either side of the equals sign are the same.

estimate To take a good guess.

expression A math idea that is not being solved (there is no equals sign).

formula Using letters and symbols to stand for numbers in a mathematical expression or equation. Generally a formula follows certain rules and can be used to solve for any value.

inverse The opposite of something else. In math, addition and subtraction are inverses.

multiplication One of the four basic operations in math; the process of repeated addition.

operation A math process, such as addition, subtraction, multiplication, or division.

place value The value of a digit that is based on its position in the number.

regroup Making groups of tens to help make solving math problems easier.

subtraction One of the four basic operations in math; the process of taking a number away from a larger number.

unit The object that is being added or subtracted, such as rides or tickets.

For More Information

Books

Adler, David A. *You Can, Toucan, Math: Word Problem-Solving Fun.* New York, NY: Holiday House, 2006.

Lee, Cora. *The Great Number Rumble: A Story of Math in Surprising Places.* Buffalo, NY: Firefly Books, Inc., 2007.

Scieszka, Jon. *Math Curse.* New York, NY: Viking, 2007.

Tang, Greg. *Math Potatoes: Mind-Stretching Brain Food.* New York, NY: Scholastic Press, 2005.

Websites

Aplusmath
www.aplusmath.com
Interactive math resources for teachers, parents, and students featuring free math worksheets, math games, math flashcards, and more.

Coolmath Games
www.coolmath-games.com
Try your hand at games that make learning and practicing math fun.

Math Playground
www.mathplayground.com/wordproblems.html
Solve math word problems with Thinking Blocks, Jake and Astro, and more.

Index